christmas presence

rob lacey

This booklet comes wishing you a
Happy Christmas and a Liberated New Year.

christmas presence

rob lacey

GRAND RAPIDS, MICHIGAN 49530

Contents

This book is dedicated to Carol – thanks for all the great songs!

12 Days
of Christmas

On the 12th day of Christmas my true love sent
to me...

Twelve strips of tinsel,

Eleven lights a-flashing,

Ten baubles dangling,

Nine cards a-sparkling,

Eight towels a-matching,

Seven books a-flicking,

Six packs of Stella,

Five chocolate coins!

Fourteen pairs of socks,

Three garish ties,

Too many sweets

And a cheap imitation fir tree.

On the 13th day of Christmas the way it's "meant to be" ...

I shelve my decorations for

Eleven months of working

Ten hours a day for

Nine months' worth of money and a

Spate of shopping-itus, it's not my

Seventh heaven, in fact it makes me

Sick and

I've ... had ... enough!

For I want to break

Free of all this farce

To spend my cash

On some cheap stimulation for me!

Foreword

The Immaculate Misconception

Once upon a time there was a little girl who wore a long red cloak with a hood. One fine day she was skipping through the forest to visit her Grandma. But she arrived to find her wicked step mother disguised in Grandma's wig saying, "All the better to clean the kitchen floor with!" All of a sudden an angel appeared in a blinding flash of light and he huffed and he puffed and he blew the house down. As the dust settled he said, "Don't worry Little Red Maryella, blessed art thou amongst women. You don't have to mop floors with your Granny's blue rinse anymore; you *shall* go to the ball! But first you're going to have a baby – for I shall turn this pumpkin into a baby buggy."

Little Red Maryella said, "But how can I have a baby when I am not married?" The angel said, "Don't worry, Father Christmas is going to bring it down the chimney." The little girl replied, "Ooh, that sounds lovely, I'll go and tell my Prince of a boyfriend Joe Charming." Joe couldn't believe it and nearly dumped her because he thought she'd cheated on him. But he had a dream where he asked the mirror, mir-ror on the wall, "Who is the fairest of them all?" The mirror said, "You are being very fair if you marry the girl 'cos she's been fair to you, fair play." He didn't want the ugly sisters to say, "Oh, yes you did," every time she went, "Oh, no I didn't." So he played the hero and married the girl. Ding Dong merrily on high.

But the Wicked Caesar of the West decreed their honeymoon would have to be a yellow-brick-road-trip with a donkey who had no brain, to the Emerald City of David. When they got to the little town of Bethlehem it was snowing, and there was tinsel and flashing lights everywhere which strained their eyes so much that their peripheral vision began to blur, and every sight they saw had a lovely soft focus finish all around the edges.

But there was no room at the Faulty Towers Inn so the other J.C., who was wearing very long bath towels and a tea-towel on his head, sent them out through the beer garden where there was a barn full of animals. They were quite hungry by now and there wasn't much space, so they decided to eat the turkey even though there was no cranberry sauce. They had a romantic meal by the light of the nose of the reindeer who'd picked up a heavy cold due to it being the middle of the bleak midwinter.

Now it just so happens that when they got there it was Christmas Day! And Father Christmas delivered the baby, as promised, and they called him Jesus. The baby came with a holy halo kit (batteries included) and was very good and his blue eyes didn't shed any tears.

Then a saint of a shepherd with a big belly and a white beard, who was called Nicolas, turned up and gave the baby lots of presents out of a sack he had on his back – one was a fluffy sheep, but Mary thought it was unhygienic so she took it back with the receipt. An-other of the shepherds was a man called Scrooge, but he'd convinced himself that it was "the thought that counts" because he'd seen too many ghosts singing the carols of Christmas past.

Then three Kings turned up who had been following the biggest of all fairy lights in the sky. They had adapted to local culture by also wearing very long bath towels and tea towels on their heads. They told Mary they wanted to make baby Jesus into a star, so they all did a song and dance routine. Well the little dog laughed to see such fun, and the dish ran away with the spoon. They had to hide from bad King Wenceslas in an Egyptian pyramid until good King John killed him in the Crusades and Maryella and Prince Joe Charming could move back home and bring their boy up to get an A-level in wood-work – chopping down Christmas trees and turning them into tables. In his spare time he volunteered for the Good Samaritans where he helped people by telling them they'd better not shout they'd better not frown, since Santa Claus was coming to town, and so they'd bet-ter be good for goodness sake if they want to have a happy Christmas!

—© Rob Lacey and Abby Guinness

So what's the *real* story?

For a similarly short, three minute single version, go to www.thewordonthestreet.co.uk.

For the full album version, read on …

What's It All About?

True story:

I was collecting some duplicating from a High Street print shop that was also advertising their Christmas card designs. You could choose from three, incorporating either:

a a snow man with tinsel scarf,

b a reindeer and accompanying sleigh, or

c a fir tree with tacky lights on.

Two other customers were also considering the Yule Tide Greetings Cards and one guy turns to his mate and says, "Don't you just hate the way they get religion into Christmas?"

The options again?

> **a** a snow man with tinsel scarf,
>
> **b** a reindeer and accompanying sleigh, or
>
> **c** a fir tree with tacky lights on.

I was too stunned to say anything.

Now I'm not anti-slush. Every year I spend Christmas with my in-laws in Bavaria where we enjoy a picture postcard setting with a snow-snuggled town square, tinkling lights and a brass band playing "Stille Nacht, Heilige Nacht..." And, yes, I love it! I just need to not disconnect with the "why?" of it all. I guess this is my attempt – bit late for the guys in the print shop, but hey!

—Rob Lacey

Prologue

John's Voice   John 1:1-18

1-2

Nothing.

No light, no time, no substance, no matter — the Voice was there.

Before anything moved, mutated or mated, Jesus, God's Voice, was there with God from the kick-off.

How come?

'Cos Jesus, "God's Voice", is God. Before anything began, they had always been. Before there was even anywhere to be, they were there.

3-5

Jesus got the name "God's Voice" because he just spoke and stuff started. From nothing to everything, sparked only by the Voice. There's nothing that doesn't have the phrase "made by Jesus" stamped on it somewhere. His words were life itself, and they lit up people's lives — his light could blast its way into the dingiest corner, and yet the people who preferred darkness still missed it.

6-9

So God sends John Baptizer to raise Jesus' profile: to lift up the Light. His job spec doesn't exactly fill a page — it just reads, "Help people take it in and take it on". Obviously, John's not the Light: he's just there to build expectation and commentate when the genuine article makes his entrance and starts lighting things up.

10-13

And when he does? Bizarre! No one recognizes him! He speaks them into existence, but they don't recognize him or his voice. He arrives at the front door of his people, and most don't even peek out of the spy-hole to check. The few who take the risk realize who he is, open up and knock a meal together. To these guys he starts doling out adoption papers to sign them up as God's children. Conceived by *human* passion? No, by *God's* passion!

14

So God's Voice gets flesh and blood, skin and bone. He spends time with us; we hang around with him, get to know him, see what he's like. And? As magnificent, as superb as you'd expect God's only Son to be ... and heaps more! God's over-the-top gifts oozing from every pore: everything he does and says rings true.

15-18

Like John Baptizer says, "Yeah, I hit the headlines first, but *he's* the one you should get excited about. He was around well before me." And because he was so stuffed full of good stuff, we've benefited — big time. Okay, Moses gave us the Contract, but Jesus the Liberator gave us God's gifts and God's truth — loads better. Who's seen God? No one. But we've seen his only Son, Jesus, and you don't get closer than that.

Chapter One

And Finally...

Exclusive? Luke 1:1-4

1-2

Okay, so I'm not slapping the word "EXCLUSIVE" all over the front
cover – I'm not the first! There's plenty of other bios (authorised
and unauthorised) flying up the bestseller lists. Other authors have
published their take on how ancient predictions have come to life in
the Here and Now with us – most of them reliable transcriptions from
eyewitnesses and accredited storytellers who can say, hand on heart,
looking you straight in the eye, "I was there."

[Luke 1:1] "Authorised" would be Dr Luke's version, Matt's account, Mark's take on Pete's story and then, much
later, John's account. "Unauthorised" would be more dodgy versions supposedly from Thomas, Mary Mag, and
plenty of other sensationalised, semi-fictional accounts of what might've possibly happened; some of them
should be called the Jostick-Gnostic Gospels. Not that anyone would mess with the text today, surely!

[Luke 1:1 – 2] Where do we get the word "authorised" from – if it's written by an author, then it's ... erm ...
"authorised", no?

[1] **God Reps = Priests.** The "go between" for God and his people – not to be mistaken for the "get-in-between". Years back, this guy named Aaron was the very first God Rep, and since then only his family line was eligible for the post.

[2] **Religious HQ = Temple.** Jerusalem's focal point of the Jewish Religion. Literally a house for God. Question is, how much does God get let out?

[3] **Purest Place = The Holy of Holies.** The heart of the Religious HQ complex: the inner sanctum. Off-limits for all but the most devoted and then only once a year on a rota basis!

3-4

So since I'm well into this and have read around the subject, soaking myself in research, it rings true for me to lay down for you a definitive bio for you great Godloving readers: the What, Where, When, How and Why of the whole story. So you'll be convinced that the stuff you've been taught is water-tight.

Here goes…

Expecting Luke 1:5-25

5-7

Old man Zechariah is standing beside one of a series of huge billboards with the giant-sized image of Herod the Great keeping Judea's throne warm.

Quick Bio on Zechariah: One of the God Reps[1] – part of Aaron's family tree, on the branch of the Abijah family. His missus, Elizabeth, could also claim an Aaron family surname. Both of them genuinely good people in God's eyes, living in line with the Maker's Instruction Manuals. The bad news? Their branch of the family tree is about to get lopped off; Elizabeth can't conceive. Plus, they're both clocking up the years.

8-10

It's Zechariah's 15 minutes of fame, the Mount Everest moment of his God Rep career.

It's his group's shift at the Religious HQ[2] and the old God Rep dice have landed on his name – he's "randomly" picked out to do the incense-burning honours in God's Purest Place[3].

[Luke 1:3-4] The dignitary Dr Luke was writing to was a Greek name: "Theophilus." Literally, Mr God Lover.

[Luke 1:7] In first century Near East, pre-PC days, couples who can't moan about the stress of the school run are treated like they're virtually disabled. The standard knee-jerk reaction was, "No Kids = No Values". Back then, they were convinced it was God's way of saying, "Not best pleased with you!" Course we know that God's not like that, don't we?!

His colleagues, the public, everyone — they're all outside, in deep conversation with God.

It's now! His big moment. He moves into the Purest Place to burn the incense to God.

11-13

Old Zech's doing the stuff when God's top angel is standing there to the right of the Incense Altar. Zechariah's freaked! He's frozen with fear, but the angel gives it, "Whoa! Don't panic, Zechariah. The top item on your wish list to God has been stamped with the word 'ACTION' and signed off by God. Your wife, Elizabeth, is going to have your baby boy. His name? John.

14-15

"He'll be a joy-factory for you and his birthday will be party time for so many. God'll look at him and always see the caption "Great" large in the frame. He'll be teetotal — no beer, wine or spirits. He'll be crammed full of the Holy Spirit. From manhood? No. From childhood? No. From birth? No. Get this: from conception!

16-17

"He'll round up so many Jews and bring them back to God their Boss. He'll clear the way for God; it'll be an action-replay of old Elijah, turning dads' hearts back to their kids, turning rebels' ears back to the wise words of their right-living advisors. He'll get people ready for God the Boss to show."

[Luke 1:11] Question is ... does Zechariah dare to wonder if God's speaking to them again?

God's voice has been on mute for 400 years! No couriers, no memos, no nothing. Check out God's last words of the Old Testament in a proper Bible. The last memo before God pressed pause was Malachi 4:5 – 6.

So what's the message now? Is it a mobilisation order for the underground insurgents to rise up and overthrow their Roman Oppressors? Is it the rallying call for the people's revolution? Nope, it's that Zech's going to be a dad!

18

But Zechariah comes back at Gabriel and asks, "And you can prove this? Face it, I'm not exactly just out of college, and my missus is no teenager either!"

19-20

The angel lays into him. "Have you any idea who I am?! Gabriel's the name. I've got an all-access pass to God's heaven! I'm delivering this message to you personally! And you have the nerve to interrogate me? You won't say one more word until all this has played out its natural course and the baby's gurgling away."

21-22

Shift scenes to God's Religious HQ, just outside the Purest Place. The crowd are nudging each other, raising their eyebrows, palms, shoulders asking, "What's keeping him?"

He steps out, and all he can do is mime. They realise, "It's some sort of visitation." "He's had a vision!"

23-25

Zechariah ties up the loose ends and clocks off duty. He goes home. Then Elizabeth gets pregnant, but keeps it on the quiet for five months. But she's convinced, "God's done this for me. He's proved he's for me by operating his shame-ectomy procedure and giving me my baby. From now on no one will look down at 'Old-Mrs-No-Kids'."

Luke 1:26-38

26-28

Second time in six months, God sends his top angel on an "overseas" trip: Gabriel picks up his work order for the day. It reads, "Destination:

[Luke 1:23 – 25] Would Elizabeth's Psalm 23:1 read, "The Lord is my Gynaecologist ... he leads me besides broken waters..."!?

[Luke 1:24] So why does she keep it to herself? She must've been bursting to tell her neighbours, family, anyone – she's pregnant! At her age!

[Luke 1:26 – 28] Does God have "bad books"?

Nazareth, Galilee County. Contact: Mary, fiancée to Joseph Davidson. Special note: she's a virgin."

Gabriel wings it up to Nazareth and hits Mary with the line, "Hi! D'you know what? You're in God's good books! God's with you."

29 – 33

Mary's emotions are churned up, thoughts flying round her brain trying to get a grip on what's going on. But Gabriel cuts across her short circuiting thoughts with, "Whoa! Don't panic! Like I say, you're in God's good books. Here's the plotline: you'll get pregnant, have a baby boy, call him Jesus, he'll be Great! Like, Son-of-God Great. Like, Invited-To-Sit-On-David's-Throne-By-God-Himself-Great. Like, Running-Jacob's-Whole-Family-Line-Of-Jews Great. Like, No-'Best Before'-Date-On-His-New-Nation Great. We're talking Divine God level of Great. We're talking none other than The Liberator."

34

Mary comes back asking, "Uh … er … um … exactly … uh … how am I to have a baby? You know I'm a virgin, yeah?"

35 – 37

Gabriel tells her, "It'll all be down to God's Holy Spirit: you'll conceive under his shadow. The Pure Child you'll give birth to will go by the title 'God's Divine Son'.

[Luke 1:28] How does Gabriel manage to relate to both ends of the generational spectrum? Mary could've been as young as 13. Bit of a gap from his last official visit to Old Man Zech. Does he change his approach? Or just tell it like it is?

[Luke 1:29] Were Isaiah's words on the tip of her tongue? Didn't every Jew know the classic line predicting The Liberator? (Isaiah 7:14 in a proper Bible): "Therefore none other than God Himself will give you the stomping great big clue: A virgin will get pregnant, she'll give birth to a son, and she'll call him God-With-Us."

[Luke 1:29 – 33] Was Gabriel wishing he'd brought his lead trumpet from the band for this announcement? Or did he deliberately choose to underplay the Big News?

[Luke 1:34] So how come Old Zech got "muted" for answering back to an angel and Mary gets off scot-free? Or does Gabriel pick up a difference in tone, gesture or body language? Or is it 'cos she's only about 13?

The Jews News Interviews

Local girl in miracle baby claim!

The locals up in Nowheresville Nazareth are up in arms over a teenage pregnancy with a difference. The mum-to-be, Mary Davidson, is making the controversial claim of what some are calling Divine Insemination. Outraged neighbours are calling for Ms Davidson to be stoned, but others think there might be something to her "miracle baby" story. We talked to the girl at the centre of the controversy.

JN — Mary, thanks for giving us this exclusive. Well! What's it feel like?

MD — Weird! Wonderful! Both ... somehow at the same time. I mean, what Jewish girl hasn't brushed her hair while dreaming of being pregnant with The Liberator? I mean, most pregnant women wonder what their child will be. Boy or girl? Rich? Famous? But it's weird actually *knowing*! It's a boy and he's the one to liberate us.

JN — From the Roman Occupying Forces, right?

MD — If that's the big thing we need liberating from then, yes, I guess that's top of God's list.

JN — So are you ready for all the celebrity? Your life's not going to be the same. You know that don't you?

MD — No, I suppose not. It's not really sunk in yet.

JN — And it won't all be "congrats, Mary". Are you aware of the gossip flyi round which, shall we say, questions the parentage of your little baby?

MD—Yes, it hurts, but I can't stop it. I'm not exactly going to make this up, am I? Not when it's just asking to be labelled a ... well, you know what. Not when they're going to call my boy a, uh ... all sorts of names!

JN—And, we hear it's all the rage in your family, this "miracle baby" thing?

MD—Yes, my cousin Elizabeth's also expecting, also a boy! She's, like, oh, fifty or sixty years older than me – I've never asked – so hers is just a bit amazing as well. I just hope she's not feeling as sick in the mornings as I am! Not at her age! Something's really going on.

JN—Yes, but *she's* married. And her hubby's not exactly a toy boy either! How's it been with the hardliners campaigning to have you, uh, dealt with by The Good Book?

MD—Well, I switch: sometimes I'm scared stupid; sometimes I get this image of stones flying at my skull and they've got my name on each one. But I've got to try and pull the plug on that. Most times I just think if God's got plans for the boy, then who's going to damage the mum? Then the stones seem to curve past me, like I've got some sort of force field or there are angel bodyguards throwing themselves in front of me and taking the fire.

JN—You're a brave girl. And how d'you see the nipper dealing with the inevitable playground rumours and nicknames?

MD—I have thought of that. Nothing's private in a village this small. And kids are cruel, but he'll know he's special. And maybe the bullying will be the making of him: help him get inside the head of picked on people. Maybe it's all part of the plan, if he's going to liberate us from the Roman bullies.

"What about your cousin Elizabeth?" Gabriel asks. "And how old is she? Yes, Elizabeth, who's had to carry the label 'Old-Mrs-No-Kids' – now six months and showing! Proof that God's vocab. doesn't include the word 'impossible'."

38

"I'm at God's service!" Mary says to him. "Bring it on, bring it all on! Just like you said."

Gabriel leaves, mission accomplished.

"Family Tree" Matthew 1:1-17

1

For the record: "The Family Tree of Jesus 'Liberator' Davidson. True Jew. Abraham's Boy."

2-6

Abraham Terahson is Isaac Abrahamson's dad, who is Jacob Isaacson's old man, who is called "Papa" by Judah Jacobson and his 11 brothers. Judah marries foxy Ms Tamar and they become ma and pa to the Judahson boys, Perez and Zerah. Perez calls his nipper Hezron, who calls his lad Ram, who goes for the name Amminadab when he has kids. Amminadab Ramson lands on the name Nahshon, who grows up to have Salmon, who gets together with that (in)famous lady

Don't Like This? [Matthew 1:1 – 17] Just skip it. Most do. Say, "Who needs family history? Just give me action."

[Luke 1:36] Did Mary not know Elizabeth was pregnant till Gabriel spilt the beans? Did this miracle turbo drive her conviction levels?

[Matthew 1:1 – 6] Anyone with a Jewish head would be replaying great stories of most of these characters. They're more than names; they're bedtime stories; they're playground role plays; they're Saturday School tales told by their favourite class teacher. It's like the Jewish mind has a whole series of drop-down menus from which they can select scores of great stories (blockbusters, soaps, epics) and song lyrics from their proud national heritage. Surnames are important these days.

[Matthew 1:5] Hey, how come there are women in this family tree? Isn't that a bit PC for these times? Maybe in Greco-Roman culture, but not in their culture! And what women?! Iffy or what? Tamar was a Canaanite, Rahab was a prostitute, Ruth was also a non-Jew and Uriah's widow Bathsheba was involved in an extra-marital affair with King David. What sort of God uses such dodgy people to produce a New United Nation of Israel?

Rahab to produce Boaz. And it's foreign girl Ruth who lands Boaz and they call their lad Obed. This is the Obed who grows up to have a nipper called Jesse who is granddad to King David's children when the famous King marries Uriah's widow and has Solomon Davidson with her.

7-11

Solomon is paternal unit to Rehoboam, who's daddy to Abijah, who likes the name Asa for his baby boy, who goes for the longer name of Jehoshaphat for his offspring (which can be shortened to Jeho if the boy thinks it suits him better). Jeho (shaphat) gives his boy the option of having the same shortened name as his dad by calling him Jehoram, who obviously doesn't like it 'cos he calls his little one Uzziah. Uzziah has a tot and calls him Jotham, Jotham has an Ahaz, Ahaz has a Hezekiah, who brings up Manasseh, who raises Amon, who does his bit to make Josiah, who produces Jeconiah and all his brothers. Quick time check? We've arrived at the Babylon Eviction[4] (around 600 BC). Fast forward 70 years...

12-16

Once they're back home we pick it up with Jeconiah having baby Shealtiel, who grows up to have Zerubbabel, who fathers an Abiud, who sires an Eliakim, who produces Azor, who creates a Zadok, who makes an Akim, who names his ankle biter Eliud, who's always liked the name Eleazar, who chose Matthan for his crumb-crusher, who went retro with the name Jacob for his kid, who followed suit with the name Joseph for his little man, who got engaged to Mary who gave birth to Jesus Josephson ... aka Jesus Davidson ... aka The Liberator.

[4] **Eviction = Exile.** Posh word for "kicked out" from the Hebrew verb "to uncover" or "to remove" into captivity. "Home" was a big word back then too.

[Matthew 1:7 – 11] But it's all sliding downhill from here: Again the Jewish mind throws out graphic images of this era ending with Jewish slaves being carted off to Babylon City. Horrific scenes of the history-changing national disaster – which you'd not want to maximise to full screen – sending a shiver down any Jewish spine. Not the most visited part of the Heritage Programme, but a vital time in their history.

[Matthew 1:12 – 16] The Jewish mind gets to feel more positive with these roll calls: King Cyrus of Persia "liberating" the Jews and letting the people buy a single ticket back to Jerusalem. With Zerubbabel rebuilding the rubble of Jerusalem and the Nation getting back to something approaching Solomon's "good ol' days".

Don't Like This? [Luke 1:39-41] All this baby leaping malarkey! Call it coincidence or old/young wives' tales! Work out the statistical chances of this happening and then snort in a derisory fashion. Build in favourable assumptions about baby John being an active baby in the womb, which would increase the random chance of him leaping on Mary's entrance. That should just about scupper the spooky inference that the foetal John "sensed" Jesus enter the room. Yeah, as if!

17

So, 14 generations of a family tree from Nowheresville with Father Abraham to the Great Kingdom of David. Then 14 generations diving back down from David to the ultimate low of the Babylon Eviction. Then 14 generations from the end of the Eviction up to The Liberator.

Mums united Luke 1:39-45

39-41

Mary packs her necessaries and heads south (70 miles/110 km) to Zechariah's house in the sleepy hill towns of Judea. She makes straight for her cousin and says, "Hey! Cuz!"

Elizabeth hears Mary's voice and inside her, pre-baby John nearly leaps through the wall of his mother's womb. Elizabeth's filled to spilling point with the Holy Spirit.

42-45

She's splurting out, volume cranked right up, "How happy are you?! Of all women, just how ecstatic must you be?! How special is this tiny baby inside you?! But whoa, how big is this? You come to me! The mother of my God comes round to my place? The second I heard your voice, baby John did cartwheels to kick off the party! You are so happy to be convinced of what God has said will happen."

Mary's big single Luke 1:46-56

46

Mary improvises and says, "My soul is a magnifying glass for God.

47-55

"My spirit is a joy-machine working overtime for God my Liberator.

It's like he's only thinking of me!

It's like he's only focused on me his worker, his menial task coworker.

From here on in, history will mark me down as the happy Mrs Happy of Happyville.

[Luke 1:41] Does baby John hear Mary's voice, or does he sense cousin Jesus is only yards away – just the other side of two sets of skin?!

For the Potent God has worked incredible things for me. He's purity itself. He's outstanding!

Ah ... the way he gives out the slack – for the young, the middle aged, the old, all the generations – all the nations for respecting him.

Ah ... the way he waves his hand and the draught blows the arrogant off the scene for neglecting him.

Ah ... the way he pulls thrones from under the rear ends of kings.

The way he escorts the modest into high profile things.

Ah ... the way he nourishes the poor, those wasting away, with food that gives life.

The way he shows the rich the door, how he waves the rich away from the buffet of life.

The way he's always been with Israel – giving out so much slack, from today right back to Abraham and his boys, right down to now, right down to ever, and farther.

The way he said he would, to our fathers.

The way he said he would, to our fathers."

56

Mary settles in at Elizabeth's for about three months.

Then she goes back up north, to home.

Don't Like This? [Luke 1:46-55] Just harden yourself to the emotive power of music. Write it off as manipulation through the overuse of the string section. Even better, conveniently forget that this is poetry and interpret everything literally, which makes it suitably unbelievable!

[Luke 1:47-55] No, Mary's not some 13-year-old singer/songwriter prodigy. Rather, she's adapting a song she'd have known well from Saturday School at the local religious HQ in Nazareth. She's improvising around some classic words of poetry from 1,000 years back by Hannah – like Elizabeth, another lady with infertility struggles in pre-IVF days. Hannah got her "miracle baby" – Samuel, kingmaker for David, 1,000 years before. And now Mary's expecting the ultimate "miracle baby" – The Liberator himself. So she's playing around with Hannah's words and injecting them with energy and exhilaration. For the original lyrics, check out 1 Samuel 2:1 – 11 in a proper Bible.

John's delivery Luke 1:57-66

57-58

Soon after Mary leaves, Elizabeth's baby's due. She has the boy, and it's party time! All the locals – extended family, neighbours, the whole community – are bubbling over with the way God's given Elizabeth a break. They're thrilled for her.

59-60

One week and one day later, they're at the circumcision ceremony in the local religious HQ[5]. The order of service is all written up with the family name "Zechariah Abijahson" written into the space for the "BABY'S NAME".

Elizabeth blurts out, "No! Wait. Sorry, um, his name's going to be ... well ... John, actually!"

61

"John?! John?!" they blurt out. "Who in the whole dynasty of Aaron has ever been called something as, well, sorry, but common as ... John?"

62-64

They make signs to the baby's dad to get his take on it. Zechariah's miming, "Notepad, bring NOTEPAD. Urgency!"

And with multiple chins hitting the HQ stone floor he writes, "H-i-s n-a-m-e i-s J-O-H-N."

On the final stroke of the letter "N" his mouth's in gear again, and he's spouting off about how brilliant God is.

[Luke 1:59 – 60] Babies have always been named after cultural heroes – it's just that there weren't so many Old Testament couriers called Britney or Justin back then.

[Luke 1:60] Outrageous! Okay, so she's a "woman of a certain age", but it's still out of line for a woman to speak out and name the child. But what's she to do, when her husband's tongue-tied?

[Luke 1:62] What's with the sign language? Was Zechariah deaf as well as mute? Seems that way.

[Luke 1:62 – 64] Wondering if Zechariah tried to mime the name "John" before he went for the notepad option. Particularly iffy for the North American reader!

---

65 – 66

The locals are blown away and the rumours bounce around the hill towns of Judea like billiard balls. Everyone who hears the news chews it over with the incisors of the heart: typical lines are variations on, "Who's this lad going to be?" 'Cos, no question, God's got his vision locked onto this boy – to do him good!

Zech's big release Luke 1:67–80

67

John's dad, Zechariah, is bursting out with Holy Spirit energy. He gushes,

68 – 69

"Celebrate God, Israel's God:

'Cos he's bought back his people from their liberty loss.

He's turned up and shown the people-stealers who's Boss.

He's bought back his people from the confidence shakers, the hostage takers.

He's gone to great lengths to erect a great symbol of strength.

Plastered it all over hoards of billboards around David's place.

A strong symbol of Liberation: blatant, strong and in-yer-face.

70

"(God's old couriers[6] hand them the mic; let them say what they like. They'll say, 'Hey, we told you, told you it'd be this way!')

[6] **God's Courier = Prophet.** Personal message delivery service direct from God. Think any package delivery corporation, but think "quick". Although, thinking about it, with their record, the depot for uncollected packages would've been pretty chocka by the end of the Old Testament.

[Luke 1:67] What might Zech have blurted out? Possibly, "Listen, all I did was ask a question!" Or "Right, now you listen to my side of the story." Or even, "I'm suing that Gabriel for defamation of character. Especially if this ever gets written up into a book!"

But no, only good things to say!

[Luke 1:68] Is Zech some stream-of-consciousness lyricist? Is he a creative genius who can write top song lyrics off the hoof? Maybe, but like with Mary's song, this could be him improvising around standard phrases – creating a remix version of previously released material from old time poets. Check out Isaiah 9:1 – 7 in a proper Bible for the sort of cracking lines that would've been a major musical influence on Zech the singer/songwriter.

71

"Liberation – from the nation that occupies, the nations that tyrannise.

Freedom – from the grabbing hands from foreign lands.

72 – 77

"All designed to remind us of promises, contracts with our history, with the forefathers of you and me.

The promises he made on oath with his main man Abraham.

Promises of respite, of civil liberties despite our enemies.

Promises of Religious freedom, of license to burn our incense in purity and integrity.

And here, baby John, you bundle of potential:

You'll move on to help people take it in and take it on;

You'll step up to become a League Number One courier of God.

You'll be the trailer, the compeer, the emcee to build expectancy, to get agnostics off the shelf, off the fence, before the main act – God himself makes it all make sense.

You'll be an educator, running crash courses in Liberty, workshops in Being Free.

You'll be an instigator, sorting out their mess by getting people saying yes to God.

78 – 79

"All this because the tenderness of God goes easy on our mess.

His scorching sun rises and compromises the shadow of death's dark cowl.

His rising sun warms away our cold, dark world with heaven's rays, and guides our wandering ways onto paths of peace.

Guides our wandering ways onto paths of pure release."

80

As the boy John notches up the inches on the doorframe, his height is only outgrown by his spiritual stature. He makes his HQ out in the wasteland until it ticks around to "going public time".

The Jews News Interviews

Old Man Zech breaks his silence

It's some people's secret wish – a Religious Leader with nothing to say! But in Zechariah Abijahson's case, it was an angel visitation which struck him dumb. Now the new dad's got his voice back, so we sent Ben Fischer to see what he had to say.

JN — So Rabbi, you were unable to speak for more than six months after a freak happening in the religious HQ! Tell us about it.

ZA — Well I won the toss to go into the HQ proper. I'm doing the stuff and, weird, I'm not alone. I look round and there's this – I don't know – guy: big shining, telling me Liz is going to be pregnant.

JN — And you said. . .?

ZA — Well, I made some wise crack and that was the last line for about six months.

JN — So, let's get this straight. You were in the hot spot of Religious HQ and you didn't expect God to talk to you.

ZA — Well, no I. . .

JN — And even when you saw a heavenly messenger you still weren't convinced?

ZA — No. It'd been over four hundred years since any one had heard anything so. . . I just didn't. . .

JN — And then baby John comes along and your lips unzip?

ZA — Yes. And I'm a different guy!

JN—So I suppose you're talking 24/7 now, yes?

ZA—Well, no, actually. It's not a bad discipline to be forced to shut up —it's like an extended silent retreat. Can't tell you the number of times in the last nine months where I would've given someone the benefits of my learning, only to think, later, what an intrusion it would've been. When you really think things through from every angle, you often take a totally different tack from your first knee-jerk ideas.

JN—So will you be going back to all your parishioners with some well-thought-through advice for them?

ZA—Some, but I won't be going to most of them, since actually all they wanted was someone to tell—get things off their chest, feel listened to. They've probably worked it out themselves by now.

JN—So you'd recommend this for all Religious Leaders then?

ZA—Well, I wouldn't advise anyone to talk back to an angel, especially not Gabriel himself! I think I got off lightly—could've been much worse. What *was* I thinking?

JN—Thanks for the tip.

Chapter Two

Christmas Presence

Two teenagers in love Matthew 1:18-25

18-19

So, how'd it happen? Baby Jesus. The Liberator? You ready for this? I'll tell you: his mum, Mary, is engaged to Joe. They'd not had sex yet – but – weird! She's pregnant. And it's courtesy of the Holy Spirit.

Pull focus onto Joe – a good guy, trying to do the right thing, and he's desperate to keep this news off the grapevine channels. The locals would come down so hard on her. He's working out how best to deliver the "sorry, but it's off" speech – without the gossip grapevine crashing from overload.

[Matthew 1:18] You sitting comfortably? You won't be soon: this is not the sugarcoated version of Christmas we've all come to love/hate/survive (delete as applicable). This is Christ-mas with no extra additives. Chew it over!

20 – 21

He's smashing the billiard balls of his best options around his brain, well into the early hours. Finally he drops off and God downloads a dream: An angel's saying:

"Joe Davidson, don't bottle out of making Mary your wife. I'll tell you why. 'Cos it's the Holy Spirit's baby. She'll have a boy, and you'll put the name Jesus down on the birth certificate. Why 'Jesus'? 'Cos it means Liberator, and that's what he's going to do for all his people ... liberate them from all the mess they've gotten themselves into."

22 – 23

Look it up! It's exactly what God got his courier Isaiah to predict years back. And I quote:

"Step back! Get your head around this headline: 'Pregnant Virgin!!' Virgin girl will get herself a baby boy who'll answer to the name 'Immanuel', which everyone knows means 'God's with us'. "

24 – 25

Joe wakes up and, yes, realises it was all a dream. But he follows his Angel Orders to the letter and the wedding's back on! Joe and Mary still don't have sex till the boy's born. Joe makes sure the birth certificate reads, "First name: Jesus".

[Matthew 1:20] Why did an angel actually put in a personal appearance for Mary and Zech, but only had a walk-on part in one of Joe's dreams? Would it be harder, and therefore more impressive, if Joe acted on just a dream, not an actual angel sighting?

[Matthew 1:21] Joe would've known that Jesus is an ethnic Hebrew variation on Joshua – like David is Dai in Welsh, and John is Juan in Spanish or Jean in French. So was Joe getting flashbacks of stories of Joshua back 1400 years ago, finishing off what Moses had started?

[Matthew 1:24] Two names then? "Jesus" – a typical, normal, no fanfare, everyday name. And "Immanuel" – an outrageous, controversial, surprising, brand new, fresh out-of-the-box, no previous owner type of name. Which would he choose to go by in later life?

Delivery suite 38b Luke 2:1-7

1-3

Meanwhile, in the depths of the Roman Empire, he-who-must-be-obeyed, Augustus Caesar, announces the Big Count-up. Caesar the Big Cheeser wants accurate population stats across the Roman Empire at the time when Quirinius is in the Syrian governor's mansion. Everyone is expected to trek back to their hometown for registration.

4-7

So Joe Davidson sets off on the 80-mile (130 km) trip down the map from Nazareth, County Galilee in the north, crossing the border to Bethlehem (aka Davidstown), County Judah in the south. He takes his fiancée, Mary, who's pregnant and showing. Three, four, maybe five days later they arrive and realize someone else is about to cross a border and arrive – her waters break. Crisis! "No Vacancy" signs in every B&B window. Decision. Mary has a "home birth" in a livestock shed. She wraps strips of cloth round the baby and uses an animal feeding trough as a cot.

[Luke 2:1] Quick Bio. Augustus Caesar was the adopted son of Julius Caesar. He'd wiped out the A-list celebrity figure of Marc Antony in 31 BC (whose main publicist was William Shakespeare – only 1600 years late!). Now Augustus has created a personality cult, setting himself up as "World Liberator/Saviour". Anyone spot a power struggle in the making? Add to this the fact that he talked up his adoptive dad as divine and much of the press pumped out the line "Augustus, aka Son of God". Mmm, sparks could fly!

[Luke 2:4 – 7]

"Noisy night, chaotic night. All is alarm, all is fright.

Rounded virgin now mother to child. Wholly infant, so Other, so wild.

Awake at an unearthly hour." (x2) © Joe Davidson

[Luke 2:7] No vacancies? Why didn't he pull in some family favours – it's his hometown after all! Or were family ties a bit frosty with the rumours flying round? Was this "Do It Yourself" stable birth a result of the Davidson clan's collective cold shoulder? They're on their own and whatever Joe's "involvement" in the "women's work" of childbirth, can't help wondering if the words of Micah were ringing round his ears. Check out Micah 5:2 – 5a for this 700-year-old prediction. (Don't check it out if you want to leave things as a surprise!)

The Jews News Interviews

Carpenter delivers!

Handyman Joe was used to making deliveries, but mostly household furniture from his Davidson Designs workshop. Here he tells Jews News how he delivered his own baby ... or was it someone else's?

JN — So, Joe, Caesar's population census couldn't have been timed worse for you?

JD — It wasn't ideal, but I was proud of being a Davidson and loved going down to Bethlehem. But, no, taking Mary at nine months' pregnant wasn't great timing!

JN — Bureaucracy, eh?! So you just rolled up your sleeves and got on with all that yucky stuff?

JD — What other options were there? Leave her to get on with it? Hope an angel gynaecologist turns up with his heavenly forceps?! I wasn't even the dad – we'd not had sex – but hey...

JN — So "stepdad" just had to step in! Did you expect a little more help from the locals?

JD — The irony was that I couldn't play the "Baby Immanuel" card. The angel told me, but what am I to do? Say, "I'd really appreciate en suite facilities since my wife's expecting God's predicted Liberator – I'm sure of it, 'cos an angel told me ... in a dream"? Like that's really going to open some doors! Not.

JN — So you really believe this little lad Jesus is going to be The Liberator?

JD—Hey, if you can't trust the girl you love, then who can you trust? Plus the angel dream backing up her story. If you're going to walk through your local shopping centre with your arm around the subject-of-all-gossip, you've got to be pretty convinced.

JN—Only "pretty convinced"?

JD—Well, 'course, I've lost sleep thinking, "What if the dreams were—you know—just too much cheese before bedtime?" But you've just got to take it on the chin. Besides, I know Mary! The Good Book says it's got to happen to someone, why not her?

JN—Why not exactly! Will you promise to come back and let us know how he's taking shape? Maybe he could write a regular column for us, when he's older.

JD—Maybe, yes. You can get me on www.davidsondesigns.bis.is.

JN—You're a brave man.

[1] **Shalom = Peace/Serenity.** Just one of the best words ever! Hebrew for peace and wholeness. Oh, and completeness. Throw in soundness and neighborliness, and you're nearly there. Just needs a bit of well-being and security and finish off by adding honest dealing and true justice. Not bad for a six-letter word (or, in Hebrew, a three-letter word plus optional assorted dots!).

Abandon sheep Luke 2:8-20

8-12

Pull back to the fields outside the (overpacked) town, focus in on a local Sheep Security Team sitting through their night shift.

One of God's angels turns up, with brilliant supernatural special FX packing the fields with God's radiance. The guys are scared stupid!

The angel delivers his standard "Don't panic!" line, then hits them with, "I've got great news, great news to bring a smile to every shape of face on the planet. Mark the date in your diaries! Today over in Davidstown there's a new baby born. Not just any baby – *the* baby! The Boss, Liberator God himself, turning up for you in baby-shape. You'll know which baby – he'll be wrapped up snug and lying in a feeding trough caked with old animal grub."

13-14

Cued to make their entry on the last line of the breaking news, the whole angel choir turn up and blast out the song:

> "Celebrate his worth.
> Elevate the God of heaven's worth.
> And on planet Earth, serenity;
> In your earthly home, shalom[1];
> For all who have known God's smile.
> For all with a God-pleasing lifestyle."

15

Once the angel choir scoots back up to Heavenly HQ, the Sheep Security Team come out with, "Let's check it out." "Yeah, let's hit the

[Luke 2:8] When the angel picked up his work order and read his speech, did he baulk at the bit marked "recipients of message"? Did he have the same prejudice as most well-to-do people back then – that shepherds were dodgy, unreliable characters? Did he question why he was to set up such lowlifes as key witnesses to the Big Event? Did he check the "animal feeding trough" line wasn't a typo? Or do angels never question orders?

[Luke 2:13 – 14] Question is, how long had the angel choir been rehearsing this track? Just recently when they went to the state of "high alert" in heaven? Or was it part of their repertoire since Adam and Eve's rather costly snack?

town." "Search the whole of Bethlehem for this baby." "God's putting us in the picture – let's go!"

16-20

They leg it and, sure enough, they track down Mary and Joe, then find the baby in his makeshift cot. The next days they fill the pubs with echoes of what they'd been told about this baby. The public pulse is breakneck pace as "Liberator Talk" bounces round the walls of the town. The reactions range from amazed to, well … amazed!

And Mary's reaction? She's quietly storing all this away in a safe place in her heart, bringing memories out whenever she has some space to wonder.

The Sheep Security Team go back to work, talking up God for letting them in on the whole adventure which had played out just the way the angel had said when he got them ahead of the game.

Old people's eyesight Luke 2:21-38

21

Eight days on, the Davidson family sort out the Religious and legal side of things by getting Jesus circumcised. The baby's formally registered with the name the angel had given him before he was even a lump in her belly – the name Jesus.

22-24

On Jesus' 40th day "birthday", ie, when Mary was ritually "clean" again (in line with Moses' Instruction Manuals), Joe and Mary cuddle the baby up to Jerusalem (5 miles/8 km north

Don't Like This? [Luke 2:16-20] Not so convinced that the message gets priority delivery to people who probably couldn't even sign their name? If it helps, imagine that the sight of the baby inspired them all to take literary classes and become upstanding characters who went off to college, graduated to more respectable jobs and became, well, nicely middle class. Happier now?

[Luke 2:22] Just how poor were this Davidson family? According to Moses' Instruction Manuals, they had options on what animal to offer up to God on Mary's first baby. Rich families were to sacrifice a lamb; poor families two doves or two young pigeons.

Is this our not-so-subtle clue as to why Jesus ended up always fighting in the corner of the poor?

of Bethlehem) to present him back to God. (It's all in there in The Good Book[2], Exodus 13:2,12. "Every first male baby is to be set apart as God's.")

They also do things by the Book in the sacrifice department, by making the Religious offering of, quote, "either a pair of doves or a pair of young pigeons", unquote.

25–28

Now Simeon is one of Jerusalem's "silver citizens". He's a totally together and right-living guy and only interested in one thing: relief for Israel. God's Holy Spirit is close with Simeon. He'd already had a Holy Spirit communiqué that he'd not die till he'd seen God's Baby Liberator – so now the Holy Spirit is tipping him off to be there the same time as Jesus' dedication. Joe and Mary bring Jesus in for the legal business and the old codger cuddles the baby and calls out to God,

29–32

"Whoa! This is it God! I'm at your disposal and I'm ready to go peacefully. Bury me a happy old man! You said it – you've done it! I've seen your Liberator, an eye-opener for outsiders, the pride and joy of our nation. I'm happy. Take me now!"

33–35

The Davidsons are stunned. Simeon wishes ma and pa well, and he's got a PS for Mary: "This is going to impact everyone, one way or the other – pulling them up or knocking them down. I'm talking controversial. He'll expose people's thought bubbles; he'll uncover hidden attitudes. It'll be a sniper's bullet through the soul for you, mum."

[Luke 2:25] Want the full picture of what Simeon's up on his ageing toes for? Get hold of a proper Bible – flick to Isaiah 40:1–5 and verse 9. Oh, and Isaiah 49:6 is a cracker too!

Not connecting? Okay, what if you knew that Isaiah wrote around the time when the Jews were refugees in a strange culture? What if you imagine your homeland occupied by enemy forces, so you were a virtual refugee in your own hometown? Connecting now?

[Luke 2:33] Why? Why so stunned? Haven't they realised what's going on? Or are they still catching onto all this baby will grow up to do?

[2] **The Good Book = Old Testament.** The bit of the Bible they had in first century Judah. Aka God's Instruction Manual. **Don't Like This?** [Luke 2:33–35] Skip this. Focus on the image created by more recent PR teams – the "gentle Jesus, meek and mild" persona. Soon the "controversial, dangerous Jesus" will conveniently disappear off the character radar screen. Phew!

36-37

There's also a crinkly old woman courier for God, Anna Phanuelson, a true blue Jew of the Asher dynasty. Quick bio: back before most could remember, she'd been married, but her husband had pegged it after just seven years. Since then – and we're talking 84 years – she's been a permanent fixture at God's HQ in Jerusalem, often going without food so as to be 100 percent focused on talking up God and talking with God.

38

Old Anna makes a beeline for the Davidsons and gets vocal, thanking God for the baby, going off on superlatives for all those in the crowd who were looking forward to the days of God buying back Jerusalem from the enemy.

Eastern Astrologers Matthew 2:1-12

1-2

So, Jesus is delivered in Bethlehem, Judea while King Herod's keeping the throne warm.

Same time, a crack team of Eastern Astrologers – boffin types – turn up in the capital Jerusalem with questions.

"Where's the new royal nursery, and the baby-sized King? We clapped eyes on the star with his name on it; we did the calculations back in

Don't Like This? [Matthew 2:1-2]. Not sure about a major plot development in the story being based on people reading things into the stars? Well, just write it off as Eastern New Ageism and you should be fine. Better still, just tell it to groups of little children and don't think about it too much.

[Luke 2:36] How old was she? Over 100? Depends which text you dig up. Some say she was 84. Others that she was a widow for 84 years plus 7 years married plus what, say, 16 years as a girl before getting married … equals, urm, 107? Let's just say she was old: 1, 2, 3 … "She was old."

[Matthew 2:1] How come Herod's on the Jewish throne? Being only a half-Jew and not being descended from King David makes him doubly not qualified. Did he have the constitution changed so he could progress in his career as Control-Freak-Tyrant-Type?

[Matthew 2:2] And what's with this astrology/onomy business? Was this a miraculous intervention from the God who set the stars spinning like a game of cosmic frisbee? Or was this a natural phenomenon? Astronomers have done their sums and they reckon Halley's Comet was around 12 BC-ish, which'd be too early. So was it a star getting all excited and going all supernova on them? Or maybe it's the conjunction of "the royal star" Jupiter and "the Jewish star" Saturn, which they reckon was around 7 BC? Whatever, they saw something and took it as a clue.

the Far East, and we've been foot-to-the-floor ever since to join the celebrations! Where is he, this Baby King?"

3 – 5

King Herod's thrown.

All Jerusalem's thrown at The Throne being thrown.

Herod calls an emergency meeting with his "Religious Expert Advisory Committee for Herod" (aka REACH), made up of Top God Reps[3] and Religious Law Enforcers[4]. One point on his agenda, the question, "Where's The Liberator supposed to arrive?"

The Religious Leaders know their stuff and fall over each other to quote him the 700-year-old line of God's courier[5] Micah:

6

"Okay, Bethlehem, I know you've got an inferiority complex. You may be a small noise in Judah, but the one who's going to run the Nation will be a Bethlehemite. He'll be a role model for Israel."

7 – 8

Herod calls the Astrologers back in for a private meeting, makes all enthusiastic, asking them for details on the first sightings, etc. before sending them down to

[3] **Top God Reps = High Priest.** The main man, the head honcho responsible for all the people's spiritual health. His job description states he's the middleman between God and the people; a "go between" for all negotiations … in both directions. No pressure then?!

[4] **Religious Law Enforcers = Teachers of the Law/Scribes.** Experts in Moses' law. Academics, who sadly, often became "academic" in the sense of "irrelevant".

[5] **God's Courier = Prophet.** Personal message delivery service direct from God. Think any package delivery corporation, but think "quick". Although, thinking about it, with their record, the depot for uncollected packages would've been pretty chocka by the end of the Old Testament.

[Matthew 2:3] Why? Well, Jerusalem's thrown knowing that when The Throne's thrown then tempers get thrown and principles get thrown out the window as people get thrown into graves.

[Matthew 2:5] See Micah 5:2 in a proper Bible.

[Matthew 2:6] So if the star stops over Bethlehem, how come the star-spotters go to Jerusalem? Was it that they were sooo convinced it was a royal planet they were tracking, that they assumed Jerusalem was the place? Did they not have a copy of Micah in their back pocket then?

[Matthew 2:7] Just how worried was Herod? Just vaguely twitchy or off-the-scale paranoid? Whatever, he's too polished a political animal to let the Astrologers spot any stress. But had they heard Herod's reputation for killing sprees? Did they know what they were dealing with here?

Bethlehem. "Go find him and report back – I'll need to know where I should go and join in the party celebrations."

9-10

The new boys in town make for Bethlehem. The attention-seeking star they've been tracking from the east stops; they work out the coordinates – right over where the lad is.

11

In danger of embarrassing themselves with excitement, they arrive at the house and see the baby in his mum's arms. They kneel, awestruck by him.

Once they recover from the impact, they open their presents for him: gold, incense oil and myrrh.

12

That night one of them gets a memo in a God-dream: "Avoid Herod like he's contagious!" The Astrologers make a detour on their return trip.

Not keen on competition! Matthew 2:13-18

13-15

Joe also downloads another God-dream (the sequel) where an angel's getting the Davidsons ahead of the game: "Go to Egypt with the family. Stay there till you get the okay. Herod's put a price out on the baby's head."

[Matthew 2:9] How did they find the new Davidson baby? A better question is how could they not, since the Sheep Security guys had blabbed off about it since the first night.

[Matthew 2:11] Which "house"? Were the new family in proper rooms by now? Had they sorted the family rift or set up on their own?

And how big is this? That the Astrologers react? Getting into the Jewish mind would show how big: check out the song lyrics from the original Davidson family in Psalm 72:10 – 15 for the full version. The catchy bit goes, "Dignitaries from lands you can't pronounce will announce their presence, and give their presents to this boy."

There's other stuff about the boy "being on the side of the sidelined, recharging the pride of the much maligned". And much more! Look it up. Won't take long.

The Jews News Interviews

Star quality!

Did you spot it? Did you look up? You couldn't have missed that humungous star hanging over Bethlehem in recent weeks. Dr F.N. Cents is one of the world authorities on star spotting and he's in town, so we tracked *him* down and asked him, "What it's all about?"

JN — So, Dr Frank, having traced this record-breaking star all the way from the land of the rising sun, were you relieved when the star finally lost its travel bug?

FNC — Well, more excited than relieved. We'd been building up for months to this. Since we first located the star. But probably not as excited as (you Jews would be) you have been building up to this since, what, seven hundred years minimum?

JN — Yes, but we've also had more false alarms than you. Probably more than you've had rice dinners.

FNC — Ah, right. I had not realised.

JN — And it wasn't anticlimactic, then, after your long road trip, that it was hovering over Bethlehem and not the more glamorous Jerusalem?

FNC — We did wonder if we had, as first, got our calculations wrong. But whe we saw the boy...

JN — Could you tell? I mean, say you'd just walked in off the street, would yo have realised this was a special baby?

FNC — Well there was no aura, no sparkling halo, so I do not know — but we had worked it out, so we *did* know. So it was goosebumps-on-your-goosebum time. All the potential of the Jewish Liberating King packed into one little bundle of skin and bone. Hands that would, presumably, hold a sword splattered with Roman blood, just curled round his mother's little finger. Lips that would kiss the future Queen of Israel, just dribbling, gurgling. Awe inspiring!

JN—So you could say, with respect of course, that the Geek Squad have turned God Squad?

FNC—Sorry, "Geek"?

JN—Never mind. It gets lost in translation.

Don't Like This? [Matthew 2:13-15] Is it a bit gruesome for you? Just stick to the cute images from the Victorian carol: "Away in a manger, no crib for a bed. The little Lord Jesus lay down his sweet head..."

Still **Don't Like This?** [Matthew 2:16] Quick dive back into verse two of the carol: "The cattle are lowing, the baby awakes, but little Lord Jesus, no crying he makes." Turn the volume up on the song and the uncomfortable truths of the real world will be drowned out ... for a while anyway.

They decide they'll skip breakfast and exit Bethlehem while it's still dark. They follow the road signs for "Egypt, Northern Africa" and stick around down in pyramid land till Herod's number is up. This asylum-seeker existence fits with old courier Hosea's line where God's saying, "Ready to round up my son, I pointed the loudspeaker down Egypt way."

16

Back in Jerusalem, Herod's fuming at being outsmarted by his foreign visitors. Playing back their conversation in his head, the boy could be anything up to two years old by now. So his troops get the order to carry out Action Plan B: Infanticide. Herod the (not-so) Great spells it out: "Kill every boy aged two and under in and around Bethlehem."

17-18

Look it up: Jeremiah Hilkiahson saw it all coming. His ancient poem proves it:

"Listen up. Hear that wailing coming out of Ramah Town?

Shrieking, screaming, a scraping of the soul.

[Matthew 2:13] Question. Did the Davidsons sell the gold in the markets of Egypt for the down payment on a pad? Did they keep the incense for the Religious HQ once they returned? Did they keep the myrrh burial oil for any deaths in the family?

[Matthew 2:15] How long do the Davidson's hang around in Egypt? History books tell us that Herod probably dies about five or six years later, so does Jesus start speaking with an Egyptian accent?

[Matthew 2:16] How many boys is this? It could be at least a dozen from a small town like Bethlehem. Depends how wide Herod circles his red line on his wall chart. If it was big enough to include Jerusalem up the road, then Herod was giving orders for more like a couple of hundred toddler boys to die.

[Matthew 2:17] Just how does a human being become so desensitised to be able to kill so easily? Herod's secret graves include his own wife, a whole generation of Bethlehem baby boys, and the movers and shakers of Jericho (a deathbed order from Herod to ensure there's tears at his own funeral!). Just how does this "competitor cleansing" happen?

[Matthew 2:17 – 18] Jeremiah 31:15 in a proper Bible.

Old Mother Rachel grieving for her missing children.
Uncontrollable?
No, more. Inconsolable? No, more. Grieving for her
children who are no more."

How many Herods? Matthew 2:19-23

19-20

Big state funeral. Herod the Great is dead! One of God's angels
does another walk-on part in Joe's dream life. The angel makes
his speech. "On your feet Joe. You're taking mother and child
back up to Israel. Those set on spilling his blood are out of the
picture."

21-23

Joe makes the trip. "One-way ticket to Israel for two adults
and one child, please." But he gets word that Herod's boy,
aka Herod Archelaus, is running Judea in the south and (not
surprisingly), Joe's a bit wobbly about stoking the fire of old
family vendettas. Another dream gives him the plotline; he
tiptoes off up north to the back waters of County Galilee. They
find a pad in their old home – the sleepy nowheresville town of
Nazareth – and start putting out the "home sweet home" signs.
More old-time courier predictions getting ticked off:

"The tag on his holdall handle will read, 'From: Nazareth'."

Zitty? Luke 2:40-52

40

And the boy grows up to be a strapping lad. He's packed full
of wise lines and God's good stuff just oozes off him.

41-45

Fast forward about a decade. (Bar Mitzvah time for the Davidson lad?) It's the traditional family annual jaunt to Jerusalem

Don't Like This? [Matthew 2:17-18] How come we never sing this carol by candlelight? You know the tune … "Bad King Herod last looked out. When he'd ceased believing. / Blood and guts lay all about. / Deep and crisp and even." © Joe Davidson. Spoils things a bit, no? Especially with children around. And Christmas is for the children, isn't it?

Really **Don't Like This?** [Matthew 2:17-18] "La, la, la, la. la." Grab those earphones. Play something sweet and Christmassy: "O, little town of Bethlehem, how still we see thee lie. Above thy deep and dreamless sleep, the silent stars go by…" Keep the carol karaoke compilation pumping out the syrup and you should be okay.

[Matthew 2:19] Why does history only record rich people's dates? We know Herod the Great died in 4 BC; it's
just that we don't know how far before year zero it was when Jesus arrived. How bizarre is it that Jesus was
probably born BC?

Some calendar calamity in the Middle Ages did it. Hurrumph!

---

[6] **Flyby Festival = Passover.** A major Jewish Religious festival, like our Easter/Christmas. It celebrates God liberating their ancestors from the sweatshops of Egypt. The name derives from when the angel of death passed over/flew by Jewish homes.

[7] **Religious HQ = Temple.** Jerusalem's focal point of the Jewish Religion. Literally a house for God. Question is, how much does God get let out?

for the Flyby Festival[6] national holiday. After the party a whole posse are making their way back to Nazareth. Mary and Joe are gabbing away, assuming Jesus is with friends and family up front. After checking, no one's seen him since Jerusalem, so Mary and Joe leg it back to the Big City.

46

After three days (of panic-searching) and three nights (of sleepless fretting), they track him down to Religious HQ[7] and they're in one of the foyers — where everyone hangs out — and he's sitting there, cool as you like, with the official teaching staff. He's soaking everything up and quizzing the Big Beard Academic with his profound questions.

47-48

The whole crowd are stunned by his grip on spiritual things and the answers he's coming out with. His parents spot him and break up the seminar. "How could you do this to us?" his mum asks. "Your dad and I have been looking all over, worried sick!"

49-50

"Was I that hard to find?" the trainee teenager asks. "Didn't you work out I'd be getting stuck into my Dad's business affairs?" They have no idea what he's going on about.

51

He goes back up to Nazareth with his family and grows up. All we get is that he's not a typical teenager — he does what he's told!

His mum bundles up all these precious moments in her deepest places.

52

The boy Jesus grows through puberty into manhood, through experience into wisdom, through relationships into popularity with God and the community. Quality lad!

[Luke 2:49] Who's right about who Jesus' father is? Mary reckons Jesus' "dad" has been helping her organise the search party. Jesus reckons he's been working on his "Dad's" business. Who's right?

And...?

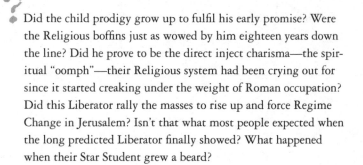

Did the child prodigy grow up to fulfil his early promise? Were the Religious boffins just as wowed by him eighteen years down the line? Did he prove to be the direct inject charisma—the spiritual "oomph"—their Religious system had been crying out for since it started creaking under the weight of Roman occupation? Did this Liberator rally the masses to rise up and force Regime Change in Jerusalem? Isn't that what most people expected when the long predicted Liberator finally showed? What happened when their Star Student grew a beard?

What did they make of him?

What have we made of him?

And why did Jesus kick his heels, working eighteen more years in Davidson Designs? Was he good with hammer and nails? Why did he wait till he turned thirty before taking a career change and going public with his "Heaven on Earth Tour"? In the "gap years" did he ever play with options on how to launch the Movement? Did he ever toy with becoming a stickler for the rules, knowing it'd get the Religious Jews on board? Did he ever role-play the highbrow philosopher image knowing it'd be a sure fire cert. to win the influential Greek vote? At what point did he ditch the option of playing the All Action Hero, knowing it'd be a 'language' both the Romans and the Revolutionaries would get? At what point did he decide to just be himself?

What did they make of him?

What have we made of him?

Why did Jesus revert to storytelling mode on the big public stages? Why did he only explain his deep-as-you-like stories to his Team Twelve? Why did he leave his uneducated public to work it out for themselves? Didn't they ever get the wrong end of the stick and miss the point? Like, what does the word "prodigal" mean anyway; like, what's so surprising about there being a *good* Samaritan—they're always lovely when I ring them; and could Jesus really squeeze a camel through the eye of a needle, and should Animal Welfare be notified?

What did they make of him?

What have we made of him?

? Who was he? If Jesus was "The Answer" how come he spent so much time asking questions? And why is it that the Movement he set up today mostly preaches and points out the answers— even if people ain't asking; even if they're asking different questions? Why did Jesus put a silencing order on most of the success stories from his Mobile Miracle Clinic? Didn't he want to milk the Word Of Mouth publicity machine or what? Why did he make it so difficult for the hangers on to sign up to his Movement: what's all that stuff about having to pick up our cross— isn't religion about "burdens falling from our backs"; what's all that about losing our lives for him—isn't religion about getting "life in all it's fullness"? Didn't he want the fringe people swelling the numbers? Didn't he realise "Numbers Count" when you're trying to change the world?

What did they make of him?

What have we made of him?

And why did Jesus put a silencing order on the demons he exorcised, blocking them from broadcasting who they knew he really was? What would've happened if the people had caught on? Who was he? Were they right? Was he really God in flesh and blood camouflage? If so, how come he chucked his global contacts list; cut up his heavenly credit cards; pulled the plug on the Dazzle Special FX; walked off without his body guards? How come he broke all the "Use What You've Got" rules of Public Relations and yet still pulled A-list celebrity crowds?

What did they make of him?

What have we made of him?

Why did most normal people take his supernaturals as proof of a hotline to God but the Religious Leaders had alarm bells going off? What was so dangerous about this guy? Was Jesus deliberately difficult? Why did he calm the lake one time and rock the boat the other? Was this pacifist trying to pick a fight? Who labelled him "a drunkard"? Who libelled him as "a nutter"? Who invited him to their parties and why? Why did he make a habit out of eating with the "wrong" people? Is that what got him killed? Who thought he was a revolutionary in the wings? Were they close? What sort of revolution was he into? Who did he turn the tables for? Did the Religious Suits have any other options on their Boardroom Table but to eliminate this subversive loose canon?

What did they make of him?

What have we made of him?

Why did he go to Jerusalem if he new it was dangerous for him? Why did he humiliate the Religious HQ Strict And Particulars? In public? How did he turn the other cheek when the soldiers were playing "guess whose fist"? Was he just a victim or could he, should he, have handled his defence better? Why did Pilate agree to him being executed Roman style? How come Christians have turned a tool of execution into jewellery to be proud of? And why's it called "*Good* Friday"?!

What did they make of him?

What have we made of him?

What kind of "Liberator" accepts the death sentence and leaves the Jews struggling under Roman Occupation? What kind of "Liberator" comes back from death and *still* leaves the Jews struggling under Roman Occupation? What's going on here? Why did Jesus exit through the ozone so soon after sorting Death and all the mess? Why did Jesus entrust the whole Jesus Liberation Movement to a bunch of a.w.o.l. losers with an iffy track record? Did he really think they could handle it? What difference has it made that his Movement is now generally part of the establishment? How ironic is that?! Does Jesus ever feel cramped working within an institution? Where d'you find him these days?

And ... what's all this got to do with Easter bunnies and chocolate eggs?

And ... why wasn't "Going to Church" one of *The Times* Newspaper's One Hundred Things to Do This Easter?

What have we made of him?

What do you make of him?

Rob Lacey, 1962–2006

Author and performer, husband and father Rob Lacey lost his coura-
geous battle with cancer on May 1, 2006. He is survived by his wife
and two young children.

Rob battled cancer on three separate occasions, an experience which
shaped his performances and writings. His book *the word on the street,*
a vivid retelling of the Bible, was awarded "Book of the Year" by the
Christian Booksellers Convention in 2004. That same year, Borders
named it one of the "Best of 2004" in the Religion and Spirituality
category.

Rob's final book, *The Liberator,* retells the story of Jesus using the
same distinctive style as *the word on the street*. *The Liberator* was
published weeks before Rob passed away.

The following is an excerpt from the tribute to Rob, delivered at his
funeral by author and pastor Gerard Kelly…

Rob's passion was to see the church use words more fluently and more
artfully… [He] brought an unstoppable energy to performance that
was exhilarating to see…

[Rob's] books, and the live performances that have been adapted
from them, have brought the rhythms of an ancient story alive for
hundreds of thousands of people on both sides of the Atlantic. They
have changed the way we think about communicating biblical truths.
Rob was a pioneer, and he knew it. He was out on a limb; skating on
thin ice; pushing things as far as they would go and hoping, praying
that others would follow close behind.

And they did. Performers, poets, writers. Those who worked with Rob or for Rob remember him as a passionate leader who had a knack of seeing the best in all of us... As much as he longed to walk the high fields of creativity for himself, he wanted others to walk them too—to discover the artist within each of them... Because alongside loving words, Rob loved people, and he loved to see people enjoying and expressing their God-given gifts. If you are one of those people—if you have been on the receiving end of the challenge and encouragement that Rob brought—then you know what to do to keep his memory alive. Write. Paint. Dance. Sing. Cook. Sew. Enjoy the creativity your Creator has wired into you. Don't let the flame die for want of exploration and expression. Honour Rob by continuing to honour the gifts God has given you.

So Rob is remembered as a great writer and performer, and as a leader of others. And even if there were nothing else, that would be enough. But there is something else... Rob had a glorious, generous, Technicolor, sky-wide picture of the character of God. The God Rob had come to know was so beautiful, so gracious and loving and kind and forgiving and good. Rob wanted more than anything that we should know how good God is. And the more he immersed himself in Scripture—the more he dived down deep into these ancient texts to bring up their treasures for the rest of us who stood waiting on the shore, the more he wrestled with how to get it across—the more he was convinced... of the beauty of God.

It was this that sustained him in his battles, one-on-one, with the terrors and the pains of cancer. It was this that gave him hope and comfort; it was this that kept him going: that the God he prayed to was and is the God of Adam and Abraham, of Miriam and Moses, of Deborah and David and Mary and Jesus and John. The God who weaves himself into the joys and pains of the poetry of scripture was and is Rob's God—and he is good. This was Rob's discovery. This was his joy. And nothing—not pain, not cancer, not even death—could rob him of it.

Rob stumbled upon the most remarkable secret of them all. The curtain was held back for him. He saw the beauty of God. That was his gift, and his legacy.

We want to hear from you. Please send your comments about this book to us in care of zreview@zondervan.com.

Thank you.

GRAND RAPIDS, MICHIGAN 49530

WWW.ZONDERVAN.COM